The wondrous world of
BIRDS

The wondrous world of
BIRDS

Robert Burton and Bruce Coleman

Photography © Bruce Coleman Ltd.

First published in Great Britain in 1976
by Colour Library International Ltd.

Printed by OFSA Milano and bound by L.E.G.O. Vicenza Italy

Display and text filmsetting by
Focus Photoset Ltd.,
134 Clerkenwell Road, London EC1R 5DL.

ISBN 0 904681 12 2

Enquiries should be sent to:

Colour Library International Limited
80-82 Coombe Road,
New Malden, Surrey KT3 4QZ. Tel. (01) 942 7781

COLOUR LIBRARY INTERNATIONAL LIMITED

INTRODUCTION

Birds must be the most popular of all animals. Horses, dogs, cats, even fishes and snakes, have their followers but they cannot compete with the regular army of birdwatchers and bird fanciers who are reinforced by the irregular battalions of people who put food on the bird table, feed the pigeons in the park or just enjoy seeing birds about them. The popularity of birds must lie in their conspicuousness. Birds are easy to see as they fly, perch on trees or sit on water. Their songs and often bright plumage are designed to make them easy to see. By contrast, mammals such as mice, foxes and badgers, are furtive. They slink through the undergrowth and are most active at night. Birds are also more diverse. There are twice as many kinds of bird in the world than there are mammals and they can be found anywhere. One south polar skua lived up to its name and was actually seen flying over the South Pole. Some places are thick with birds. Lake Nakuru in Kenya is the home of hundreds of thousands of flamingoes not to mention pelicans, storks, herons, ducks, waders and kingfishers. Lake Nakuru is near the equator and there are many hundreds of species of birds to the visitor from temperate lands but as we travel towards the poles the numbers of species diminish. There is still no shortage of birds, however, and we can find huge colonies of penguins in the Antarctic and of auks in the Arctic.

What has made birds so successful? Undoubtedly it is their power of flight. The ability to fly has allowed birds to live in many places, from jungle to the ocean, and to exploit many kinds of food. Birds are travellers. They can migrate thousands of miles to breeding places where winter weather or summer drought prevent a year-round existence.

Birds are descended from reptiles but their bodies have been so transformed by modifications needed for flying that little can be seen of their reptilian ancestry. Let us examine some of the changes that have taken place in a bird's body. Feathers are the equivalent of a mammal's fur and keep the bird warm. The body has to be warm to let the muscles work at maximum efficiency. Feathers also give the bird a smooth streamlined outline and provide the flight surfaces of the wing. The wings are modified forelimbs, now capable of little else than flapping to provide the impetus for flight. The necessary power is generated by the huge breast muscles that give birds their plump figure. To help the muscles, birds have lightened their bodies as much as possible. They have lost their teeth and have a horny bill that acts as a universal tool. From the shape of the bill we can guess at a bird's diet. There is the wicked hook of an eagle, the chisel of the woodpecker, the fishing net of the pelican, the probe of the oystercatcher and the stout conical bill of seed-eating finches. Bills are also used as weapons in disputes between birds and for all the delicate tasks of nest-building and preening the feathers. Internally, weight is saved by the thinness of the bones and the reduction of the tail to a stump that carries the tail feathers. To guide its flight, a bird must have good senses and quick reflexes. Vision is particularly important. The falcon must keep track of its prey as it dives at nearly 300 kilometres per hour, the owl has night vision 100 times better than ours and migrating birds navigate by detecting minute changes in the position of sun and stars.

As well as being flying animals, we think of birds as being animals that build nests. Nests help to keep the eggs and nestlings in place while the parent birds keep them warm by incubation. There are two main kinds of nesting habit. Some birds build elaborate cup-shaped nests or nest in tree holes and burrows in the ground. Their eggs hatch into helpless nestlings that have to be fed until they are old enough to fly. Other birds make no more than a scrape in the ground. Their babies can run about and feed themselves soon after they have hatched. A few birds do not make nests. The emperor penguin of the Antarctic holds its single egg on its feet and the cuckoo lays its eggs in the nests of other birds.

The 8,000 species of birds come in many sizes and shapes. Each one is perfected for a particular way of life. The ostrich is flightless but runs fast on its long legs; the penguin is also flightless but it uses its wings – now turned into flippers – for swimming. Albatrosses have long narrow wings for gliding effortlessly over the ocean; vultures have broad wings for soaring over the African plains. Swifts chase insects on their narrow wings; they even sleep in the air. Herons and storks have long legs and necks and fish in shallow water. The variety is enormous. Even the largest and most learned book cannot possibly give all the details of the lives of birds, even if they were known. All that can be done in a small book is to show some examples of the way that birds live. Some birds have seemingly bizarre habits but on investigation they prove to be the means by which the bird is exploiting a source of food, shelter or some other need. Other familiar birds lead what we think of as normal lives yet, when we get to know them better, they reveal habits just as interesting.

In the following pages, facts about the way birds live come to light by examining selected kinds. We look, first of all, at birds in flight, then the way that they bring up their young. Two particularly interesting kinds of birds are the birds of prey and the waterbirds. The birds of prey hunt other animals for a living. They must always be on the alert for prey so that they can pounce unawares. Waterbirds feed on the rich variety of plant and animal food to be found in fresh and salt water. Some stay near the edge and just paddle. Others go into deep water and dive to great depths in search of fish. Finally, we look at a variety of birds, familiar and unusual, each of which has its particular point of interest.

Birds in Flight

The three pictures on this page show a common European starling flying to its nest and feeding its youngsters. The starling is a most successful bird. It eats a wide variety of foods and has become so abundant that huge flocks settle each night to roost in cities or in the countryside. Because of its pretty colouring and ability to mimic, the starling has been introduced to America and Australia. The flight of the starling, and that of any bird, can be compared with the flight of an aeroplane. A bird's wing combines the functions of both the wing and propellor of the aeroplane. Its shape is an aerofoil: thick and blunt at the leading edge and tapering to a fine trailing edge. This shape reduces the pressure of the air flowing over it and creates lift, which keeps both bird and plane airborne. The beating of the bird's wing increases the lift and also propels the bird forward; the strong downstroke thrusts the bird upwards and forwards.

Straight and level flight is relatively uncomplicated but take-off and landing poses problems. A plane attains its flying speed by accelerating down the runway but most birds leap into the air with a thrust of the legs and a gigantic downbeat of the wings. Until it is properly airborne, the bird angles its wings so that it gains lift on both up and down strokes but this is very tiring and it settles to the easy rowing motion of forward flight as soon as possible.

When they land, both bird and plane have to slow down yet maintain as much lift as possible so that the shock of hitting the ground is reduced. As the bird comes in to land, like the starling here, its body becomes almost vertical while the tail and wing feathers are widely spread to act as air brakes. The wing beat is changed so that the bird is 'back-pedalling' but also gaining lift so that it sinks gently and does not fall out of the air. The primary wing feathers are splayed out like fingers and each one acts as a miniature wing. On approaching the perch the bird 'lowers its undercarriage' by throwing its feet forward. During flight, the legs have been tucked up in the feathers to aid streamlining but they now form a shock absorber to take up what remains of the bird's momentum and cushion the landing. Immediately on landing the toes grasp the perch and the claws are forced in to hold the bird firm.

The honeyeaters *(top left)* are a family of small birds living in Australasia and the Pacific Islands, as far east as Hawaii. They are nectar eaters like the hummingbirds, sunbirds and honeycreepers. All these birds are extremely agile in flight as they have to hover or land on the flimsy petals of showy tropical flowers before they can insert their long tongues into the flower.

The movement of the honeyeater from one flower to another helps to pollinate the flowers. The honeyeater picks up pollen on its feathers from the stamen of one flower and brushes it onto the stigma of another.

The barn owl *(bottom left)* is like a ghost. Its white form shows up dimly in the darkness of the night as it flies on uncannily silent wing beats. Like the other night-hunting owls, the barn owl seeks its prey by the use of acute vision and hearing. The owl can pick out a mouse sitting on the woodland floor in conditions that we would call pitch dark and can still hunt in absolute darkness, when even sensitive instruments record no light, because it is guided to its prey by its ears picking up the faintest rustles and squeaks. The owl has to fly silently if it is to hear properly and so that mice and other small animals are not alerted by its approach. Its feathers are especially soft to deaden the noise of its wing beats.

The little owl *(top right)* is a native of Europe, Africa and Asia and has been introduced into Britain. It nests in holes in trees or walls and sometimes uses burrows in the ground. Relatives of the little owl include the burrowing owl of America which digs tunnels or uses the abandoned burrows of mammals, and the elf owl of south-western United States and Mexico which uses woodpecker holes, sometimes in the giant Saguaro cacti. These owls have longer legs than most owls and often run after their prey, which consists mainly of insects and worms, as well as small mammals and birds.

The woodpeckers, *(bottom right)* like this great spotted woodpecker, are strong fliers and can be readily identified as they fly through the woods with a characteristic undulating flight of three to four rapid wing beats followed by a glide. They spend much of their time perched on tree trunks when they search for insects hiding under the bark or burrowing in the wood. The woodpecker chisels them out with hammerblows of its strong bill. Meanwhile it supports itself on its stiff tail and hangs on with its feet which have two toes facing forwards and two backwards.

Gulls *(left)* live around the coastlines of the world and they make use of currents of air eddying around cliffs and sea walls, even off the tops of large waves, to keep them effortlessly in the air. A ship is, in effect, a moving cliff and the air currents around it allow gulls to hover near the stern while they wait hopefully for something edible to be thrown overboard.

The terns *(top right)* are first cousins of the gulls. They are smaller and their forked tails have earned them the name of sea swallows. The fairy tern is one of a group of small tropical terns called noddies. It lays its single egg, very precariously, on the branch of a tree, placing it in a slight depression to give it some stability. Noddies swoop down to the sea to pick small fish near the surface and they gather where diving birds or predatory fish are forcing other fish to the surface.

The snow goose *(bottom right)* lives in the Arctic and is closely related to the grey-lag goose from which our domestic geese are descended. Water-birds have an advantage over landbirds in take-off and landing. They do not have to leap into the air nor brake hard to land gently. They can taxi over the surface of the water, running and flapping hard until flying speed is reached. On landing, the feet can be thrust out and used as brakes as the bird 'water skis' to a halt.

The lesser black-backed gull *(left)* is but one of many gulls that live around the coasts of the world. Many also live inland, like Franklin's gull of central North America that never sees the sea, but only a handful, like the kittiwake, spend much time out to sea. Gulls are good gliders, although not so expert as the albatross, and their streamlined shape is said to have inspired the design of the Spitfire fighter.

Puffins *(above)* whizz through the air like bumble-bees, their small wings flapping fast to support their stout bodies. When they leave their burrows at the cliff top they launch themselves into the air and plummet towards the sea until they are flying fast enough to level out. Puffins and other auks swim under water, using their wings.

The razorbill *(right)* is an auk that nests among rocks and in crevices of sea cliffs. Sometimes it nests on ledges with guillemots. The chicks leave the nest before their wing feathers are fully grown. They flutter down to the sea where they are joined by their parents and the families swim out to sea. The adult razorbills feed their offspring until they can fend for themselves. Before this happens, the adults moult their wing feathers and become unable to fly. However, they can still swim after fish.

Nest and Young

Garden warblers *(top right)* are summer migrants to Europe, having wintered in Africa. Their journeys are hazardous for, apart from the natural elements, millions of them, and other summer migrants, are shot and trapped in countries over which they pass for so-called sport, and cooking pots. Those that survive the journey settle down to nest in May.

In the breeding season wood warblers *(centre right)* inhabit mature woods, particularly those containing beech and oak trees. They are summer visitors to Europe turning up in April to start breeding in late May and early June. The female builds a domed nest of leaves, bracken and grasses to lay her usual six to seven eggs.

Wood warblers can be separated from their close relatives the willow warblers and chiffchaffs by their larger size, brighter yellowish-green upper parts and sulphur-yellow throat and breast and white belly and a yellow stripe above the eye.

When the swallows *(bottom right)* arrive from Africa, one is aware that spring is on the way. These attractive birds are faithful to their nest site, returning year after year to the same rafter, barn or shed. Before man arrived on the scene and provided buildings, swallows must have nested on cliff ledges.

When opened, the large yellow mouth markings of this well fed young starling *(opposite)* helps in eliciting a feeding response from its parents, who know exactly where the food has to go. Starlings start nesting in April, making use of holes in trees and buildings. They build an untidy nest of grass and straw.

Our picture *(below)* shows one of the 54 different species of flowerpeckers. This one is found in Australia and because of its liking for berries, especially the sticky fruit of mistletoe, it is called the mistletoe bird. It is a striking bird with a dark shiny back and a red throat, chest and rump.

The flowerpeckers are distributed throughout the Oriental and Australian regions – eastern China, India, the Philippines, Malaysia, New Guinea, the Solomon Islands, Australia and Tasmania. They are active, plump, short legged birds and tend to be solitary or in pairs but they will frequently attach themselves to flocks of other birds. Flowerpeckers have a preference for keeping to the high forest where they feed on berries, flower nectar and some insects.

The female builds a small, pear shaped nest beautifully woven with spiders' web, plant down and grasses.

Marsh warblers *(left)* are very difficult to distinguish from reed warblers except by the song which includes a wide range of mimicry. In fact marsh warblers are very good at miming some of the songs of the reed warblers.

In Britain the breeding population has been drastically reduced by the destruction of their wetland habitat and of osier beds, which has been brought about by the decline of basketmaking.

Both the male and female help in building the nest, the female doing the major share. It is not such a deep nest as the reed warbler's and is secured by "basket-handles" to supporting vegetation or bushes. There are usually four to five eggs laid in June. The young are fed on a variety of insect life, particularly green caterpillars and beetles.

The blackbird *(below)* is one of the commonest and most familiar birds of our gardens and woodlands. It has been estimated that there are at least ten million pairs in the British Isles alone and they are also widely distributed throughout Europe. Breeding begins in late March when they build a nest lined with dry grass and in which they lay four to five bluish-green brown flecked eggs.

Great tits *(top left)* and blue tits *(right)* are birds that can easily be encouraged to nest in the garden by simply providing them with a nest-box. Blue tits tend to lay large clutches of seven to fifteen eggs and nests containing twenty eggs have been found. Both species of tits feed their young on insects and larvae, particularly caterpillars.

Robins *(centre left)* can be similarly induced to nest by placing an old kettle in a hedge or other well sheltered spot. Here they will build a nest of leaves and moss lined with hair, and lay between four to six whitish eggs with heavy reddish freckles. The young robins do not develop the familiar red breast of their parents until late in the autumn of their first year.

The cuckoo *(below)* does not build a nest or rear its own young. It selects a host to take on this task. A female cuckoo produces from four to five eggs over a period of forty eight hours. Each egg is laid in a different nest and the female cuckoo is careful to remove in her beak one of the host's eggs, before replacing it with one of her own. After hatching, the young cuckoo begins to eject the eggs or young of its host so that it receives the undivided attention of its 'parents'.

The reed warbler *(right)* is a sombre coloured bird but it is soon identified as it works its way up and down reed stems making a churring 'chirruc' song. The deep nest is built above the water line round three or four reed stems or other water loving plants. The young reed warblers are exceedingly skilful in climbing amongst the stems of reeds and it is amazing to the observer that they so rarely fall in the water.

By the very nature of their habitat, birds which live by the water have to ensure that the nest is safe, dry and warm. The grey wagtail *(top left)* usually nests in a hole or on a ledge above, or close to, water. As the picture shows, this wagtail is more colourful than its name would suggest. A resident throughout the year (unlike the yellow wagtail which is a summer visitor to Europe) this bird may be seen around lakes, rivers and, especially, fast flowing streams.

The little grebe, or dabchick, *(below left)* builds a floating raft of water plants on which to lay its four to six white eggs. When hatched the young travel on the backs of their parents. As the parents submerge to look for food the chicks bob about on the surface of the water waiting for their parents to reappear. This small grebe likes to live amongst the thick vegetation of ponds and lakes but it is soon located by its trilling call.

Egrets and herons are colonial nesters. Very often the large, bulky nests *(top left)* are conspicuously built high in trees, well out of the reach of predators. Nesting in large numbers like this has certain advantages for the survival of the species. It affords, for example, protection against enemies – safety in numbers – and the location of food by one member can be beneficial to the whole colony. There is also evidence to substantiate the theories that colonial nesters find mates more easily and that life in a colony is sexually more stimulating. The egrets and herons feed their young on a variety of creatures such as fish, crabs, shrimps, frogs, insects, lizards, mice and even snakes.

The osprey *(bottom left)* is one of the most widely distributed birds of prey in the world, and one of the most attractive. It is a fish catcher, and is to be found hunting around coasts, lakes, rivers and reservoirs. It catches its prey by hovering over the water, or by gliding up to a height of a hundred feet or more, then diving, with legs extended and wings half closed, to almost submerge itself. On surfacing it struggles to lift itself from the water with a fish firmly secured in its talons. During the breeding season the catch is taken back to the large nest of sticks where it is fed to the young. The nest is usually built high in a tree, and some ospreys have even been known to choose the top of a telegraph pole as a nest site.

The wandering albatross *(right)* is the world's largest flying bird with a wing span of between eleven and twelve feet. It sails on these long, rather stiff wings over the waters of the Southern Hemisphere through some of the most turbulent weather that can be found. Only when mature enough to breed does it return to the isolated oceanic islands where, after courtship, it will lay a single egg and incubate it for nine or ten weeks.

Adult flamingoes *(far right)* carefully scoop up mud with their beaks, and use this to form a 'mud pedestal nest' which the hot tropical sun soon hardens. The single white egg is laid in a depression at the top and is incubated by both sexes for about a month. Within three or four days of hatching, the flamingo chick is capable of leaving the nest to wade and swim with other young members of the breeding colony.

No garden lawn would be complete without the familiar, bouncy song thrush *(centre right)*. The nest of this bird is constructed from leaves, grass, wool and moss which is then lined with mud. These nests can be found in a variety of places such as trees, hedges, garden sheds and even on the ground. The four or five blue, black spotted, eggs are generally laid from March onwards and later the young are fed on a diet of insects, slugs, worms and snails.

Nightingales *(bottom right)* are sombre brown birds with a rufous tail and rump but what they lack in colour they certainly make up for with their beautiful explosive song. They spend a lot of time singing not only during the day but also at night. Nightingales tend to keep to thick damp undergrowth and this is where they nest. The nest is built close to the ground and the four or five eggs are incubated for two weeks.

The secretary bird *(top left)* must have acquired its name from the crest of feathers on its head and neck which resembles the old quill pens that clerks of bygone days used to place behind their ears. This long-legged hawk is quite unmistakable as it strides across the African plains in search of locusts, rodents, lizards and snakes. The prey, once located, is killed by a quick thrust of the bill, or by a blow from the bird's powerful feet, and is taken back to the young at the nest, usually situated on the top of a tree or bush. Small prey is normally fed straight to the chicks but larger prey is processed and stored in the crop before being presented to the chicks in the form of a regurgitated liquid.

There can hardly be a more remarkable sight when visiting the deserts of south-west America and Mexico than to see the familiar American cartoon character, the roadrunner, *(centre left)* in a real-life dash through the cactus country. They can run at extraordinary speeds, and there is some evidence to support estimates of twenty miles an hour. These birds seem to play a similar predatory role to the African secretary bird, feeding on snakes and lizards and despatching them with powerful attacks with their beaks and beating them on rocks. The roadrunner, or chapparal cock, is not a hawk but a cuckoo which builds its own nest, usually in a bush or cactus, where it lays three to six chalky white eggs.

The destructive but attractive wood pigeon *(bottom left)* starts breeding in earnest in August and September, just when the cereal crops are ripening ready for the harvester. This shy bird of the countryside has defied all attempts by farmers to reduce its numbers, and has now successfully penetrated the suburbs and towns where it is tame, and quite approachable.

In the last century the green woodpecker *(right)* was also known as a 'yaffle', a colloquial word meaning to bark, mutter or 'make the sound of a green woodpecker'! The laughing call of this woodland species reveals its presence as it makes its way around and along tree trunks and branches. The nest is a hole bored into a tree trunk, but no nesting material is used except for a few wood chippings. Five to seven white eggs are usually laid.

Waterbirds

Many birds get a living from the sea. Some, like the gulls and terns, live around the coasts but the auks, albatrosses, penguins and petrels spend their lives in the open ocean and come to land only during the breeding season. Characteristically, the seabirds gather in colonies to breed. Colonies of little auks in the Arctic sometimes contain over a million pairs.

The fresh waters of the world also form the home of many birds and some kinds can be found on both salt and fresh water. We think of ducks as living on ponds but there are sea ducks like the eider. On the other hand, gulls, which are properly seabirds, sometimes live on lakes and reservoirs.

Some of the best places to find waterbirds are swamps and marshes where the dense vegetation provides plenty of food and shelter. Unfortunately many of these places are being drained and some of their inhabitants are becoming rare.

The mute swans shown here are one of the most familiar of waterbirds. They have an exemplary family life. Both parents defend their offspring, the cygnets, fiercely and the family stays together after the cygnets can fly.

Flamingoes *(far left)* stalk gracefully through the shallow waters of salt or soda lakes in the hotter parts of the world. Their strange curved bills are used to strain food from the water. Some flamingoes feed on microscopic plant life that forms a sort of thick soup in the lake while others catch small animals such as brine shrimps. The beautiful pink colour comes from substances in the food.

The lesser black-backed gull *(left)* is one of the many gulls that has taken to living inland as well as on the coast. It is a native of Northwest Europe where it nests alongside the herring gull. The latter originated on the Atlantic coast of North America and spread to Europe. The two are so closely related that they sometimes interbreed and produce fertile offspring.

The egret *(bottom left)* is a kind of heron and there is no real distinction between the egrets and herons. Indeed, this great white egret is actually called the great white heron in some places. This species is found in the warmer parts of five continents but one turned up on the sub-antarctic island of South Georgia, 1,500 miles from the American mainland. During the breeding season egrets are adorned with long white, lacy plumes. At one time these were so popular as 'aigrettes' in ladies' hats that egrets nearly became extinct. Their plight was the direct cause of the formation of bird protection societies.

The wood ibis or yellow-billed stork *(top right)* is found throughout the lakes and rivers of East Africa. It can often be seen with head fully submerged and wings almost fully outstretched as it hunts for fish, frogs and water insects. The lakes of East Africa are some of the best locations to spot this attractive species and very often it will be found mixing with other water loving birds such as heron, egrets and pelicans.

The wood ibis nests colonially in trees constructing the nest of sticks in which it lays two or three whitish or greenish-whitish eggs.

Pelicans *(right)* live in lakes and in the sea. Their bag-like bills are not for storing fish but for catching them. The pelican plunges its bill into the water and it opens out like a large scoop net. Flocks of the great white pelican fish together, swimming in a semi-circle to drive the fish together. The brown pelican of America is unique in that it dives for food.

The roseate spoonbill *(top left)* is the only American member of its family. It takes its name from the broad flattened bill which is used to sieve small fish and crustaceans from the water. When feeding, the spoonbill holds its bill vertically in the water and sweeps it from side to side. Spoonbills have been hard hit by the demands of the millinery trade and by drainage of marshes. The European spoonbill used to breed in England until the marshes were drained in the 17th Century.

The anhinga or darter *(right)* is a freshwater relation of the cormorant seen perched among the spoonbill. Darters live on the rivers and lakes of America, Africa, Asia and Australia. As they may swim with only the kinked neck and head showing, they are sometimes called snakebirds. Darters catch fish by impaling them. The sharp bill is thrown forward by the sudden straightening of the neck. The fish is then shaken off, caught in midair and swallowed.

The alternative name for the jacanas *(bottom left)* is lily trotter. This is a very appropriate name because jacanas walk over waterlilies and other floating plants using their long toes to spread their weight. The nest is so flimsy that it may sink as the jacana sits on it. The eggs and later the chicks are carried under the parents' wings and so kept dry.

Mute swans *(top right)* are not as silent as their name would seem to imply. Anyone who has approached their nest will know that they hiss and snort aggressively. Apart from vocal sounds their wings, when the birds are in flight, produce a quite musical humming. Mute swans may be seen on a variety of water habitats; rivers, lakes, large ponds, canals and, in the winter, on the open sea. They are primarily vegetarian but they also eat insects, frogs, toads and even ducklings.

The bitterns are small herons with relatively short necks and legs. They are found all over the world; this little bittern *(bottom right)* comes from Africa. They live in thick growths of reeds and sedges, slinking furtively and rarely showing themselves. When disturbed, a bittern points its bill skywards. This makes it difficult to see but it also allows the bittern to get a better look at the source of disturbance. Like most birds, its eyes are on the sides of its head and it cannot see directly ahead. But with its head raised it can turn its eyes down and look under its 'chin'.

Easily recognised by their conical, striped bills, puffins *(left)* are one of the ocean-living auks. The clifftops, when their burrows riddle the ground like a rabbit warren, are deserted outside the breeding season. The feet of puffins are armed with strong claws which they use to excavate their burrows but they also take over burrows dug by rabbits and shearwaters. Puffins feed on small fishes, such as sand-eels, and they can carry up to forty at one time to their chicks. Unlike young razorbills, guillemots and auklets, the young puffin stays in its nest until it can fly properly.

The cattle egret *(top left)* is unusual in feeding mainly on land while the other members of the heron family are dependent on water. This youngster shows the shorter legs which have probably resulted in a terrestial rather than wading way of life. Another interesting feature of the cattle egret is its amazing spread across the world. It lived originally in Africa and Asia but it has crossed to Australia and America. The first record for America is of a bird shot in Guyana in 1937. Since then cattle egrets have spread northwards as far as Newfoundland.

The name moorhen is derived from 'mere', an old English word for a pool or lake. Moorhens *(bottom left)* are found in the fresh waters of most parts of the world except Australia. The nest is a platform of reeds which may have to be built higher to avoid sudden floods. Young moorhens stay with their parents for some time. Those from the first brood of the year help to feed their younger brothers and sisters of the second brood.

Gannets *(top right)* nest on the tops of high, inaccessible cliffs and their nests are packed together. They go out to sea to feed and catch fish by plummetting headlong into the sea from heights of a hundred feet. The gannets half-close their wings and extend their necks so that the broad conical bill takes the main impact and the blow is further absorbed by the thick skull and a system of airsacs.

Terns *(bottom right)* are related to the gulls but are generally smaller and slenderer than their cousins. They are poor swimmers as their feet are too small and weak to provide adequate propulsion. Terns are, however, excellent fliers and divers, capable of plunging deep into the sea to catch fish and shrimps. One species, the arctic tern, is a record holder amongst its own kind. A chick which was ringed at its nest in Scandinavia was found to have died of old age twenty seven years later and another, ringed in Greenland, was found in Africa after completing a migration journey of ten thousand miles. The photograph shows two elegant terns aggressively defending their nesting sites.

Many of the kingfishers *(top left and right)* live away from water. They hunt insects, frogs and lizards. The kookaburra or laughing jackass of Australia is a land kingfisher that catches snakes, and the shoe-billed kingfisher of New Guinea digs for worms. Kingfishers are, however, best known as brilliantly plumaged fish hunters. The pointed bill is used to seize fish, grabbing them firmly, not impaling them as would an anhinga. The common kingfisher hunts from a perch, dashing out, hovering, then plunging headfirst. When it has seized its prey it uses its wings to 'fly' out of the water.

Kingfishers nest in holes in banks. The birds fly at a bank, striking it with the bill until they have chipped a ledge. Then they can perch and dig more rapidly. The chicks grow their feathers in waxy sheaths so their plumage is not fouled by the accumulation of fish bones and droppings. The sheaths drop off just before the young kingfishers take to the air.

The mandarin duck *(below)* is the most showy of all ducks. It lives in East Asia, including China and Japan, where it lives in pools and streams of forested regions. The nest is usually in a hollow tree and, unfortunately, the beautiful mandarin is becoming rare in the wild because of the destruction of forests.

Known in America as the arctic loon, from the old Norse name of 'lomr,' the black-throated diver *(top left)* is a magnificent bird whose incredible wailing call is one of the supreme sounds of northern latitudes. Divers breed on lakes, nesting close to the water's edge because their legs are set well back and they can walk only with difficulty. Outside the breeding season, divers retire to the sea.

The gentoo penguin *(bottom left)* is recognised by the two white 'ear-muffs'. It breeds on the southern tip of South America, on the ring of islands that surround Antarctica and on the continent itself, where the Antarctic Peninsula thrusts northwards. For most of the year, gentoos are spread through the neighbouring seas when small parties can be seen travelling together in characteristic 'porpoising', leaping clear of the water at intervals to take a breath of air. Nesting begins in spring when a nest of pebbles is made in a colony near the water's edge. Two eggs are laid and guarded closely against the cold weather. When the chicks get too big to be brooded, they stand in the nest then wander through the colony. The parents bring food for them but they will not allow the young penguins to take it without a wild chase through the colony. The chick chases its parent frantically until the latter stops and lets the chick thrust its bill into its mouth.

The grey heron of Eurasia and Africa *(right)* and the great blue heron of North America are so alike that they are often thought to be one species. The long-legged heron is a fisherman that stands patiently by the edge of the water then seizes its prey with a rapid thrust of the bill. Sometimes it searches its prey by stalking deliberately through the water. Only rarely will a heron actually swim. Terrestrial prey is also taken; worms and snails and occasional rats, rabbits and birds. The short-legged American green heron often dives for its food.

Birds of Prey

Birds of prey are a fascinating group of birds with a variety of shapes, sizes and behaviour. There are the fast-flying falcons and hawks, such as the goshawk *(left)*, fish-eaters like the fish eagle and the osprey *(below),* and scavenging vultures and kites whose appetites help to tidy up the land. Some of the falcons are so fast and agile in flight that they can catch swifts, swallows, bats and dragon flies on the wing. There are eagles that specialize in catching and eating snakes, and there are others that enjoy a diet of monkeys.

We must not, of course, forget those most attractive of hunters, the owls. There are the large varieties such as the eagle and horned owls that can deal with young deer and hares, and tiny owls such as the least pygmy owl measuring only four and a half inches that enjoy a diet of insects, and the fishing owls whose name indicates their preference in food and needs no further explanation.

Vultures perform a useful task in clearing the countryside of unsightly carcasses. Their keen eyesight enables them to locate, from a great height, any large or small dead animal. The world's vultures can be split into two groups, the New World or American vulture, and the Old World vulture of Europe, Asia and Africa.

The king vulture *(top left)* is a highly coloured and striking bird and is the third largest vulture of America. It is found from Southern Mexico to the tropical rain forests of Argentina.

The yelping, almost gull-like call of the African fish eagle *(right)* is a familiar sound on the lakes, rivers and marshlands of the African continent. Whilst fish is this bird's staple diet, it has also been known to kill flamingoes and a great number of other young water birds.

Travelling through the flat plains of Africa, one frequently comes across groups of vultures squabbling over a carcase *(bottom left)*. It is not necessary, however, to travel such great distances to see vultures. The holiday resort of Majorca boasts a population of black vultures, the largest and rarest in Europe, which may be seen, with luck, in the mountain districts of that sunny island.

Birds of prey are diverse in size and behaviour, as the pictures on these pages show. The eagle owl *(above)* is an exceedingly powerful bird with a wing span of five feet. The large yellow-orange eyes give it a fierce expression, and it is indeed fierce. It has been known to kill young roe deer and birds as large as buzzards.

Equally dramatic is the peregrine falcon *(left),* a powerfully built bird which is swift in flight. It usually attacks medium sized birds such as pigeons, crows and game, but falconers used to fly them at herons. When they stoop at their prey they can reach speeds of approaching two hundred miles an hour.

The two vultures shown opposite have unusual feeding habits. The palm nut vulture *(top right)* eats the fleshy covering of oil and raffia palm nuts and has been observed boring holes in palm stems for insect larvae. The lammer-geirer, or bearded vulture *(far right),* has a partiality for bones.

Africa's white-faced owl *(right)* is primarily nocturnal in its hunting habits and its highly developed hearing enables it to locate and pounce, very effectively, on small animals.

Both the kestrel *(top left)* and the barn owl help to keep the rat and mice populations down. The kestrel is to be seen over any open space, even the verges of motorways, hovering in one place as it searches the ground below for rodents and large insects.

The magnificent golden eagle *(right)* is a bird of the mountains and moorlands. It can be seen soaring majestically above mountain peaks on wings spanning seven feet. The adults pair for life and build a large nest of sticks, lined with grass. They frequently use the same nest year in and year out, adding new material as this becomes necessary. Depending on the locality, they feed on hares, game birds, young foxes, sea birds and a fair amount of carrion. A pair of golden eagles like plenty of territory to range over, and this may vary from eleven to eighteen thousand acres in Scotland to anything from twenty to sixty square miles in California. Golden eagles are often accused of taking lambs but usually they have died of natural causes before the eagles find the bodies.

As dusk falls, the appearance of a ghostly white shape floating over farmland is not an apparition but the barn owl *(bottom left)* out on a hunting expedition. They seem to have a regular hunting ground and have been observed 'quartering' their area every night. Barn owls nest and roost in barns, outsheds, lofts, chimney stacks and church belfries. Farmers often encourage them by providing a breeding box in a barn.

The sparrowhawk *(above)* uses the element of surprise when catching its prey, by low fast flying, slipping over from one side of a hedge to the other and without warning, pouncing on its unsuspecting prey – usually a small bird. It can also weave its way through a wood with astonishing agility.

In contrast, the buzzard *(top right)* does not have the agility of a sparrowhawk but is still capable of pouncing on an unwary game bird or rabbit. It has been known to follow a plough picking up the insects and earthworms revealed by the turned soil.

For real style a hunting hobby *(far right)* has to be seen to be believed! It is so agile that it can catch a dragonfly, swallow or swift in flight and pass it to its mate.

The tiny elf owl, *(bottom right)* no larger than a sparrow, lives in the deserts of south west America and Mexico, nesting in holes in Saquaro cactus previously made by woodpeckers or flickers.

There are over 130 different species of owls in the world. Their special characteristics are their forward-facing eyes, their large heads and soft plumage, providing them, in most cases, with silent flight. These nocturnal hunters can see and hear so well in the dark they can pinpoint a mouse moving under a carpet of leaves. Many of the large and medium sized owls will not hesitate to attack a man in defence of their nests.

The eagle owl *(top left)* is a bird of the forest of Europe, but not of Britain. Its future in Europe is so precarious that in recent years restocking from captive breeding birds has been necessary. A few introduced eagle owls in the coniferous plantations of the Forestry Commission might be worth considering as it is doubtful that such a small population would increase significantly to be a real threat to the indigenous wildlife.

Long eared owls *(right)* are not the easiest of birds to see, for they are very nocturnal and masters of camouflage – they press themselves close to a tree trunk so their mottled plumage merges well with the bark of the tree. They sometimes nest on the ground but their normal habit is to use old nests of squirrels, magpies, crows and wood pigeons.

The little owl *(bottom left)* usually hunts during the twilight hours but, very often they are to be seen in broad daylight, conspicuously perched on telegraph wires, fences, posts, hedges and walls. Almost fifty percent of the food intake of this bird is insects, particularly beetles, and they are also known to take rodents, starlings, sparrows and birds larger than themselves, such as pigeons.

Familiar and Unusual Birds

We think of penguins as living in the snow and ice of the Antarctic but only three species are confined to the Antarctic regions. Others are found around the coasts of South America, South Africa and Australasia. One lives in the Galapagos Islands, on the equator. Nevertheless, penguins are cold-water birds; the sea around the Galapagos Islands being washed by the cool Benguela Current. In changing from fliers to flightless swimmers, the penguins have undergone considerable changes. Their bodies are no longer built for lightness. The body is protected from the cold by a thick layer of fat and a dense coat of special short feathers, each of which has a fluffy 'aftershaft', that make up an insulating layer of warm down next to the skin. The wings have become stiff paddles and the feet have moved to the back of the body to help steering. To compensate for the shift of the feet, penguins have adopted a vertical stance on land and walk in an ungainly way. When they want to move fast over the snow, penguins drop onto their bellies and 'toboggan', pushing themselves with legs and flippers.

The Adélie penguin is one of the Antarctic penguins. It has to walk long distances over the frozen sea to reach its breeding colonies. The King penguin nests in the sub-antarctic. It does not make a nest but carries the single egg on its feet, as does its larger cousin, the Emperor penguin. The latter lays its egg in the middle of the Antarctic winter. The adults huddle together in the blizzards while they nurture their eggs and chicks.

The sulphur-crested cockatoo *(right)* is one of the more common parrots to be seen in zoos and petshops. Cockatoos are distinguished from other parrots by the crest which can be raised and lowered. The sulphur-crested cockatoo lives in the eucalyptus forests of Australia, where it lives in flocks. Each flock has a favourite roosting tree from which they sally forth to feed. They land in clearings to eat nuts, seeds and insects and while they are feeding sentries are left on guard to warn of approaching predators.

No one knows what the function of the huge bill of the toucans *(below)* might be. The bills are brightly coloured and surprisingly light. Suggestions as to their use include intimidating predators, displaying to rivals or mates and reaching out to pick distant fruit. All toucans, including this araçari, are fruit eaters but some species take insects and rob the nests of other birds. Their homes are in the forests of Central and South America.

The bill of the Old World hornbill *(top right)* is as unlikely as that of the toucans but their nesting habits are even stranger than their appearance. Hornbills nest in hollow trees and the female is walled in with a plaster of mud and droppings. A small slit is left so that the male can pass food to her. Safe in her prison, the female lays her eggs and incubates them. When the chicks are nearly grown she batters her way out, then reseals the entrance and helps her mate feed the chicks until they, too, break out.

The marabou *(far right)* is a grotesque stork with a pink, naked throat sac. It has the habits of a vulture and the two are often seen together on the African savannahs where they feed on the carcasses of dead animals. The marabou also catches small animals.

The cattle egret *(right)* is so named because of its habit of following cattle and other large animals to feed on the insects that they disturb. Observations show that the egrets catch more insects in a given time when following cattle than when hunting alone. Sometimes they save energy by riding on the backs of their big assistants.

The cardinal *(top right)* is named for the resemblance between the colour of its plumage and the robes of the churchman. It is one of the most popular and familiar American song-birds. The song is varied and can be heard the year round. Furthermore, the female sings as well as the male. Cardinals are spreading northwards and have reached parts of Canada.

The pheasants *(left and below left)* are birds of forest floors of Asia. The golden pheasant comes from the mountains of central China. Pheasants run well on their strong legs and can take off vertically through the trees in a sudden burst, generated by powerful flapping of their short, stubby wings and balanced by their long tails. The fast straight flight of pheasants, and their relatives the partridges and quails, have made them popular as gamebirds and they are specially reared for shooting. Many species of pheasant are becoming rare in the wild through overhunting and destruction of forests.

Chickens *(bottom right)* or domestic fowl are members of the pheasant family. They are descended from the junglefowl of south-east Asia and were domesticated at least four thousand years ago. Chickens reached Europe sometime before 700 B.C. and were first used for sacrifices and fortune-telling. Later they were prized for their eggs. There are now many breeds, some developed for egg laying, others as table-birds and a third group as ornamental birds. Of the last the Yoko-hama has a 20 foot trailing tail.

Parrots

Renowned as 'talking birds', parrots *(above and right)* are found throughout the warmer regions of the world. The family includes the parakeets, budgerigars, cockatoos, macaws and lovebirds. Most parrots live in forests although some Australian parrots live in grasslands. The strong legs with curved, needle-sharp claws are excellent for climbing amongst branches. The sickle-shaped beak is used to help in climbing and for tearing open nuts and soft fruit, as well as being a powerful deterrent to enemies.

Also known as the Carolina duck, the wood duck *(top left)* is a close relative of the mandarin but lives in North America. The wood duck nests in hollow trees, sometimes in the abandoned holes of woodpeckers and squirrels. The female incubates alone but her mate waits for her nearby. When hatched, the ducklings scramble out of the hole and fall to the ground, perhaps fifty feet below.

The mallee fowl *(top right)* of Australia must rank as the bird with the most complicated nesting habits. The eggs are not incubated by the warmth of the adult's body heat. They are buried in a pit and cared for by the male who continuously tests the temperature of the soil and arranges to keep it constant. Before the eggs are laid, he lines the pit with dead leaves. When they rot, they give off heat. If the nest becomes too hot, the male scrapes away the soil to let the heat out. If it gets too cool, he piles more sand on top to keep heat in. Alternatively, depending on the strength of the sun, the mallee fowl may expose the eggs to its rays or cover them with sand to shade them. In this way, the nest is kept at an even 92°F. over the total incubation period of eight months.

An unusual back view of a stone curlew *(right)*. Its large eyes can be seen bulging at the sides of its head. These eyes give the stone curlew good all-round vision but their main function is to see well at night. Stone curlews are inactive during the day and come out to feed at night, when their mournful, far-carrying calls can be heard.

The turkey *(bottom left)* is another native of the Americas. First domesticated by the Aztecs, the turkey was brought to Europe, then taken back to the United States by European settlers. Wild turkeys live in flocks, feeding by day on the ground then retiring at night to the safety of a tree. The cocks, or 'gobblers', are polygamous and court several hens apiece.

A favourite ornamental bird in parks and zoos, the stately peafowl *(above)* came from eastern Asia centuries ago but the related Congo peafowl was not discovered until 1936. The male, or peacock, is firstly famous for its magnificent display of loose varied feathers with their shimmering eye-spots. These feathers are known as the train and are not the tail of the bird; they spring from above the base of the tail.

Ostriches *(left)* are flightless birds which join the rhea, cassowary, kiwi and emu in the group known as the ratites. They are descended from birds which had the ability to fly but they are now runners with very small wings.

The Ostrich lives in Africa, where its range has been very much reduced. Its home is in the grasslands where it lives among the herds of antelope and can survive in desert regions. Ostriches are polygamous; each cock has a harem of hens which lay their eggs in one nest, but only the cock and one hen tend them.

The nightjars *(right)* are among the few birds, apart from the owls, which are active by night. During the day they crouch on the ground and their impeccable camouflage renders them almost invisible. When darkness falls, nightjars hunt for insects which they catch in their widely gaping bills. It is at this time that their 'churring' calls can be heard.

No nest is made. The female nightjar lays her two white eggs on the ground, perhaps amongst a litter of dead leaves. Both parents incubate the eggs and later feed and protect the chicks. Like so many ground-nesting birds, nightjars use distraction displays to lure predators away from the nest.

The nuthatch's *(top far right)* name is corrupted from 'nuthack', which describes the way it wedges a nut in a crack in the bark of a tree and hammers it open. Insects are eaten as well as nuts and seeds. The nuthatch searches for its food by hopping, with great agility, up and down trunks and branches.

Frigatebirds *(centre right)* are superb fliers; they soar effortlessly over the sea and their legs are so weak that they cannot take off from level ground. Their food comes by stealing from boobies and other seabirds, from snatching marine creatures from the sea surface and by nest robbing. The male inflates his red throat pouch when courting.

Because their feeding methods require so much skill, young frigatebirds have a long period of adolescence. They are fed by their parents for six months after they have left the nest. By practising on sticks and feathers young frigatebirds gradually learn to swoop on fishes, baby turtles and jellyfish. The long period of dependence means that frigatebirds can breed only once every two years.

Hummingbirds *(bottom right)* are one of the marvels of the bird world. They fly on wingbeats so rapid as to appear as a blur, and they hover easily in front of flowers to sip nectar. Despite its minute size the ruby-throated hummingbird migrates across the Gulf of Mexico.

If you enjoyed this book, will you help to
protect our birds by supporting the two
leading bird protection societies in this
country. Write for membership details to
The Royal Society for the Protection of
Birds, The Lodge, Sandy, Bedfordshire and
to The International Council for Bird
Preservation, The Natural History Museum,
Cromwell Road, London SW7. They will
both welcome your support and help.

PICTURE CREDITS